to Jane,
Some food for thought,

LOVE

by
Georgette Butcher

in the series
Quiet Times

Collins

FOUNT PAPERBACKS

William Collins Sons & Co. Ltd
London • Glasgow • Sydney • Auckland •
Toronto • Johannesburg

First published in Great Britain in 1990 by Fount
Paperbacks

Fount Paperbacks is an imprint of Collins Religious
Division, part of the Collins Publishing Group,
8 Grafton Street, London W1X 3LA

Copyright © Georgette Butcher 1990

Printed in England by Clays Ltd, St Ives plc

Love

A loving faithful God, who gave you a faithful loving wife, and has now taken her away.

Martin Luther

Luther is obviously writing here to someone whose wife has died. How difficult it can be to remember that God loves us when suffering strikes. Here the husband is reminded that his wife belonged to God before belonging to him, was his when a wife and still was his now that he had taken her.

This is not always easy to accept, for whatever the circumstances we miss those who are taken from us, and the pain is great. To bow our heads and accept the will of God in such a situation takes time. Luther's words "Although we cannot perceive God's will as clearly as we can see a wife" may well evoke a wry smile, but we do understand when he goes on to say that we can "apprehend his will by faith".

A loving God does not do anything just to hurt his children, and is willing to give of himself to help fill the void when he takes away someone we love. We simply have to hold on in love and trust, believing in his love and that the outworking of it is his prerogative.

The love of God is the first to be commanded, but the love of your neighbour is the first to be fulfilled.

Augustine

Augustine points out that we cannot see God but by loving our neighbour and drawing from the source of love to do so — then we see God. Fulfilling his commands, obeying his will for us, draws us nearer to God, and the closer we come, the more we love him.

To love God and to love your neighbour are commands that are intricately woven together. Neither are possible to do on their own. If we love God then we will love the brethren, we can only truly love others by knowing the love of God for us. When we learn that God loves us then we can turn with love to others, and the expressing of love to them reveals love for God.

We sometimes think that we need not give ourselves to others in any way. That our relationship with God is self-sufficient, that it can even be a secret thing. But meeting with God must always create a new interest in those who are also his. We shall be concerned for them and that concern should turn into action. It may be to give or to pray, something which will not leave us indifferent either to them or to God.

God loves a man who enjoys giving.

2 Corinthians (Barclay translation)

The person who is happy in his giving gives pleasure to God, it pleases God when he sees that we are generous with what he has given to us. Paul says that we should not give "reluctantly or under compulsion for God loves a cheerful giver".

Nowadays there are demands from all sides to give to worthy causes. The Christian may have to make a decision as to which he can give to simply because it is not possible to give to all. Some may put aside an amount regularly to be used for the work of God, others wait until a need arises. In the Old Testament we see that a regular tithe was demanded, in the New the suggestion is that we should give out of the abundance that God gives. We know that he is able to give more than enough for our needs and for us to give to others.

Many have proved that the more that is given the more is given back. We should not of course be generous for this reason, but because we give in God's name and find joy in giving on his behalf, and he loves us for it.

So then love Jesus, and all that he has is yours.

The Cloud of Unknowing

In Jesus is salvation, in him is life, through him we have all things. By turning to him and determining to serve and love him our life is set on course and all that we need is found in him.

"Remain in me, and I will remain in you", said Jesus to his disciples, speaking of the vine and the branches. Grafted to him, the true vine, we can bear fruit. Of ourselves, a branch alone, we cannot. "Remain in my love", said Jesus. "If you obey my commands, you will remain in my love." "My command is this; love each other as I have loved you."

Jesus told the disciples that all that belonged to the Father was his and that the Holy Spirit — the spirit of truth — would be given, and that he would bring glory to Jesus by taking from him and making it known to them. We have not only the great spiritual blessings of forgiveness and eternal life, but we may have his mind, his wisdom, his peace. We can do all things through him, nothing is impossible in serving him. "Knit yourself to him in love and trust", says the writer of *The Cloud*.

I love God above all things and I love God in all people.

Margery Kempe

We must not be afraid when we come up against great professions of faith and love from others, and wonder at the weakness of our own feelings and trust. That is not the time to feel inadequate and a failure. Rather should we remind ourselves that we are loved, that we are beloved of God, and the more we realize this, the more shall we respond to that love. For we all have to learn so much as we tread the Christian path. Everything does not come at once — in fact the joy of walking with God is the learning of new truths and coming to know him more and more.

It takes time to remember to look for God in other people, time to understand what it means and how it enables us to react, but as we do that, so God's love in us moves out to them. In a sense, we work with God's love in helping others and the more that we do, the more we realize that loving God is the greatest and most important thing in our life. Each day love for him will grow, and he rejoices in that love.

Love for the flock does not mean giving them ice cream on holidays.

Jean Vanier

The picture of Jesus as a shepherd is one that most people know and love. The Twenty-third Psalm brings comfort and help to many. Mostly we need the warm feeling of being loved and cared for, and the thought of being part of the flock with the Shepherd watching over us makes us feel safe. This is good, but we, too, have to be willing to take on the task of shepherding the flock.

Being an under-shepherd means caring for the flock in the way the shepherd himself would do it — knowing them by name and looking after each one in a personal way. The stragglers, the weak, those who are hurt, each needs an individual attention that can only come from a heart that cares. It means being deeply committed to whatever is our part in looking after the flock.

Ice cream is good, most think it a treat, but as Jean Vanier suggests, this is not what it means to look after others. It is too easy to give "ice cream" when we should be giving ourselves and our time to their support. It means being available; recognizing the wounds; knowing how to bring healing; being a responsible person; knowing how to love.

He loves the whole of you, just as you are.

Abbé de Tourville

Our thoughts concerning the love of God for us on a personal level can occasionally be rather strange. They probably come from the way that we have learnt about love from those closest to us. Our parents can sometimes unwittingly make us feel that love can only be given to us if we are good. Once the idea is planted we can carry it through into adulthood, and when we begin a relationship with God the idea persists even in this.

We wonder how God can love us, then decide that it must be a kind of "duty" love. He loves his people we know, but we may feel that we ourselves are unlovable or, as when we were children, we can only be loved when we are good. This means that we have to try very hard to please God, and this makes us feel terribly guilty if we decide that we have failed in some way.

God is not like that. His love is not dependent on our being perfect or in striving to please him. He does not just love a "good" part, his love enfolds every part of us, just as we are, today.

When we centre our thoughts upon God the Father, we sense
His love and fathering abilities.

Paul Y. Cho

God calls himself our Father, and fatherhood can be a wonderful relationship, but the Fatherhood of God is even better than that of any earthly father. When we think of God as our Father we think of what a father is: the love that is shown; the encouragement when it is needed; the forgiveness that is given; the support that is always available; the joy, the peace and everything that is shared. If we find it difficult to believe in such a love being for us, meditating on God as Father draws us deeper into his love and we begin to accept his love for us.

It was Jesus who said that we should call God "our Father", through him we have been born again into the family of God. This means that we have brothers and sisters, those who are also a part of the family. With them, we have the gift of the Holy Spirit within us.

We pray to our Father, and acknowledging the relationship entails accepting all that it means. Because he is God we do not have to feel inferior, for we have an inheritance, there is a place prepared for us in heaven.

Where there is no love pour in love, and you shall draw out love.

John of the Cross

Holiness and love grow together, and as the holiness of God is allowed to grow in our life so we are more able to show love to others. Holiness brings changes in our outlook and in the way we act and react to others. Because we become less sensitive to our "rights" and perhaps able to face the truth about ourselves more easily, it does not appear so difficult to give love to people around us. Where previously coldness or difficult relationships might have hurt us and caused us to turn away, we now find we have a more sympathetic understanding.

Out of this desire to be like God we then find that it is possible to love without thought of having love returned, and it is as we give that love that the miracle happens. The atmosphere changes, the situation lightens and the relationship becomes different.

The prayer of St Francis embodies these thoughts: *Lord make me an instrument of Thy peace. Where there is hatred, let me sow love; Where there is injury, let me sow pardon; Where there is doubt, faith; Where there is despair, hope; Where there is darkness, light; Where there is sadness, joy.*

Jesus's self-emptying love attained its completion on the cross . . . and was itself the human expression of the Father's love.

Ruth Burrows

It was God in Christ who went to Calvary and gave everything in the sacrifice of himself on the cross. This was the climax of a love that revealed itself by the stripping of everything except the ability to die.

It is at Jerusalem that we see the humiliation of God made Man. The betrayal — the knowledge of his friends leaving him — Peter's denial. Being taken away by soldiers — being mocked, spat on and flogged and eventually nailed to a cross. A cross which in itself was a symbol of shame.

If we want to know what the love of God is we need only stand at the foot of the cross and look at the body hanging there. We see God's holiness demanding retribution, and God's love paying the price through the death of Jesus. This is where the love of God is seen and can be understood, a self-giving love that holds nothing back, and the result of this love is that we are free. We unite with a whole community of those who have become followers of Christ, worshipping God and witnessing to salvation in him.

There is an utter peace, joy, security that comes from knowing the love of God our Father.

Ralph Martin

We first come to God because we have realized that we have a need that can only be met in him. We become reconciled to him, understanding our need to have our sin forgiven, and then determine to follow him. Along the way we become aware that God loves us; that is why we have been met in our need.

God's love, however, goes beyond our knowledge of human love. As his children — his heirs — we can expect him to look after us in every way if we put him first in our life. "Seek first the kingdom and his righteousness and all these things will be given to you as well." He will see that materially we have enough, but more than this, the knowledge that he loves and cares for us leads us on to know that he will also cope with every problem.

As we put our trust in him and look to him to undertake for us, so we have his peace and know the joy of being his. We belong to the family of God, and as his child may go forward with confidence in the security of his love.

Growing in holiness means growing in love.

Ralph Martin

We are required to be holy — God requires us to be holy. "You shall be holy, for I am holy" is what he has said. Holiness is seen on the human level as our conduct, and in God's eyes as walking in the way of salvation. It begins at conversion as we turn from our own way and determine to walk God's way. Along that way we shed those things that are displeasing to him and set out to be renewed, so that we take on God's thinking, his discernment, his love.

Within us we have God's Spirit who is at all times seeking to make us like him; to transform us into his likeness. It is this inner transformation that is the centre from which springs the conduct or behaviour which is the fruit of the Spirit.

As we grow in our knowledge of God, so our heart expands in love for him and we find a new freedom. As our love grows for him so will love grow for those around us. It seems that holiness and love are linked together, and as we grow in one so we also go forward in the other.

It is God's will that we should serve him steadfastly for love, without grumbling or striving against him, until our life's end.

Julian of Norwich

It must be true that if we say we love God then we should be able to serve him without grumbling or striving against his will. The operative word is "should" for we realize that whilst it should be possible we frequently find ourselves failing.

It is so easy to grumble about our circumstances; to pit our strength against his when we want to take a certain course, yet all the time knowing that he is in control. This means that our circumstances are the best for us whatever we may hanker after. His will, too, is the right way for us.

He bears patiently with our tantrums but it must give him great joy when his children accept his way without murmuring. If we say that we love him, how can we show this love except by trying to please him? Our love is proved by our trust and by our obedience; a trust that knows that God's care is all-embracing and an obedience that *wants* to obey because of that love. God desires that *for love* we will be constant in our service to him, and as we do so we shall find his perfect peace.

It is God's love that feeds me in the bread I eat and God that feeds me also by hunger and fasting.

Thomas Merton

To a large extent we are moulded by life as we have to live it. By the circumstances that tie us into situations and places; that cause us to be with the people who surround us; and until we have linked our life to God we fail to see any pattern.

Thomas Merton's life was not easy. Even on a day-to-day basis there were hardships, and as with so many of us, preconceived ideas that had to be revised. Yet he was all the time reaching out to God, and before his life ended he had found much that was satisfying in it.

To remember that God loves us even in the midst of dryness, pain, and deprivation, is to take all of it from his hand. To be able to take "bread" and "hunger" is to remember that he is the giver of each. Both can feed us, for by our trust and continual looking to him we can be spiritually fed. "My food", says Merton, "is the will of him who made me and who made all things in order to give himself to me through them."

Be fervent, brethren; if you love God draw all who are near to you, all your household, to that love.

St Augustine

Loving God means that we have the life of God within us. We reveal him by our attitudes, actions, bearing, and our love towards others. We show him to others by the way in which we love him and seek to please him, by the obvious commitment of our life to him. We are also committed to drawing them into knowing and responding to the love of God.

We sometimes think that we can win others for Christ only by words, something which can be incredibly difficult in the context of the home and family. Many are eventually won by seeing changed lives and appreciating a new understanding and care towards themselves. St Augustine believes that Christians should be concerned that others come to know about God's love; the suggestion being that if we have found it how can we deny this knowledge to others?

Being fervent in prayer helps the Spirit to work in lives. As we regularly pray, so is this work being carried on, not necessarily even seen until the time comes when there is a recognition of God. It can take time, and it means that we must not lose heart but must trust in God's faithfulness.

You cannot know the love of God to you without loving God in return.

D. Martin Lloyd-Jones

When we know that someone loves us we often find that love rises up from us in return. Once we know that someone is interested in us our own interest is immediately awakened. John says in his first epistle, "We love him because he first loved us". Because God has revealed his love it is natural to love him.

There are many people around us who feel themselves unloved. They may not show it, but they have the feeling that they have no real place in the world. This means that they struggle along day after day, wondering what life is all about. They do not know that they are loved by God.

Once we told people about judgement and hell and the punishment that was coming their way, but love is a greater weapon than fear. In a world where human love has become so transient the need is to reveal the strong, unchanging love of God. People have to be told that there *is* someone who loves them. That in spite of everything that they may feel about themselves, they are lovable. Only as this is understood can there be a response to the love of God.

O God of love, we pray Thee to give us love . . .

William Temple

Love is not automatic, we do not always feel love to those around us. Jesus reminded his disciples that it is easy to love those who love us, and we can expect no reward for doing so. It is our neighbours and our enemies that we have to love. It is those who persecute us that we have to pray for. We have to feel love deep in ourselves for people and their needs.

William Temple's prayer encompasses all aspects of daily living. He asks for love for those with whom we work and those with whom we play. For love in our speaking and in our thinking; surely two areas where it is not always easy to be truly loving. He mentions those who are hard to bear and those who find it hard to bear with us.

We can really only show love in such a way when we allow ourselves to be completely open to the love of God. When we let his Spirit enter our hearts and minds with his gift of love, then we can share it with those whose lives we touch and those across the world who need love and prayer.

I lost my first love.

Corrie ten Boom

Corrie ten Boom has a chapter in one of her books about the time when she made a decision to follow her own plan instead of God's plan for her. Very quickly, through an African minister, she saw that she was wrong. Once "I wanted everyone to know that no matter how deep we fall, the Everlasting Arms are always under us to carry us out." "Now I was interested in my bed. I had lost my first love."

It is easy to become complacent, to lose the first love we had for God, when we were ready to do anything, go anywhere for him. The years go by; there may be a slowing down, a loss of urgency. Like Corrie we think more of our bed than "tramping the world", whatever that may mean for us. It may come from concern about the things of the world, or losing our time with God. Temptations abound to turn us from the path.

As soon as Corrie ten Boom realized her fault she turned to God. "I confessed my sins and asked for forgiveness. And the same thing happened that always happens when I bring my sin to God in the name of Jesus: He forgave me."

The cry for love that flows from the heart of people in need is mixed with pain, anguish and sometimes agony.

Jean Vanier

The wealthy, those who have everything — health, sanity, a whole body, a family, a home — find difficulty in entering into the agony of those who do not have these things. It is not only a question of not being able to understand, it is so often one of not wanting to do so; of being fearful. We find those with broken bodies and minds too demanding, too threatening.

What must it be like to know that your misshapen body is repulsive to fellow beings? To realize that although your thoughts are clear it is impossible to communicate them in an easy manner, and so people are embarrassed? To long for love and yet believe that it is impossible to attract it to yourself?

We shower love upon a baby, and the child blossoms and seems to open up in response. It does not realize that it needs love but is able to recognize its warmth. The human heart hungers for love, it is a deep inner need, and when it is in the seemingly unlovable, what added anguish it must bring! It is impossible to think that Jesus could not but have a special place in his heart for those in such need, and that he does not look in sorrow on those who will not try to love where it is so much wanted.

But what is perfection? It is love "rejoicing evermore, praying without ceasing, in everything giving thanks".

John Wesley

John Wesley believes that as we go along the road of sanctification, going on from grace to grace to perfection, that it means having perfect love, and he identifies love as taking up the whole capacity of the soul and "rejoicing", "praying", and "giving thanks".

Out of our love for God should come praise and rejoicing, an acknowledgment of his giving causing us to give him our thanks and continual prayer. A heart of love not only desires to please but is conscious of what is owed. So this redeemed life of ours needs to reveal its love to God by a continual on-going relationship. One that spills over in joy because of being one with him, and recognizes and acknowledges the gifts that he bestows.

Praying without ceasing is a continual upholding of oneself to God and a recognition of his presence with us. It need not be a matter of words but just a thought, a remembering of him as we go about the tasks of the day. Knowing a togetherness, seeing him in the things and people that cross our path. It can mean taking the minutes to pray about his world, his work; sharing our life with him.

All my occupation now is the practice of the love of God.

John of the Cross

The mystics were always reaching out to know God. This did not necessarily mean that they did not have calls on their time but in these words it seems that John of the Cross had left much of these aside and was seeking to devote his time to showing God's love. Often we can be so occupied with things that take up time, so concentrating on the material things of life, that we fail to devote time to being what God wants us to be.

His love toward us is so great that we almost deny it when we do not in turn reveal it to other people. It is easy to forget that our need has been met in him, and that there are those who do not yet know about the love of God in a personal way for themselves.

Devotion to God means being occupied with him, basking in his presence — his love — until we are saturated, and his love is continually flowing through us. His love is seen in our acceptance of our life as it is from his hand: the practice of love. Making *that* the important part of our life, whatever else is in it.

But Christianly understood, loving is loving the very person one sees.

Søren Kierkegaard

To love is to love the person. It is not to love the good or the perfect things to be found in that person. These may help in attracting us to someone, we may admire them in a person, but a true love is able to love in spite of the imperfections. One could go even further than this and say that the imperfections are not important, it is the good and the possibilities for good that are seen, rather than anything else.

True love does not set out to change someone because what is seen is displeasing. Love is in love with, or loves what is seen. God himself does not seek to alter us. He wants us to grow and enter into spiritual understanding, to put aside the things that are wrong and sinful, but he loves the essential sort of person that we are, in spite of our imperfections.

It is not easy to love the one who brings disgrace upon us. Or to continue to love the person who betrays us in some way, abandons us or becomes indifferent, but basically it is the same person that we see and should continue to love.

We are all the time measuring God's love by ours.

Dwight L. Moody

The world measures love by how it is seen; even Christians tend to take the same viewpoint. It is easy to love when the other person appears worthy of our love, but if he fails in some way then we are inclined to want to have nothing more to do with him.

The idea has grown up that if we do something bad then we are not worthy of love, and certainly that God will not love us. If this were so then none of us could ever know God's love, for "all have sinned". The great message of the Gospel is that although we are sinners God loves us, and if proof were needed it is to be seen in the giving of his Son.

Then we think that we cannot be sure that God's love will continue towards us. That unless we are "good" he will not love us. We need only look at the disciples: how they forsook him at the crucifixion; how Peter denied him; how Judas betrayed him. Jesus did not cease to love them all, and we may be assured that God's love is steadfast, that he will not withdraw his love from us.

What is wrong with our world is that love is in short supply.

Christopher Bryant

In his book *Journey to the Centre* Christopher Bryant writes that "in heaven we shall be loved . . . by the Love that creates and recreates all things and we shall love in return". He suggests that this is not merely a love for God but a total love which will include all our fellows.

It may well be hard to imagine what such total love means. Here on earth love is flawed; it becomes many different kinds of love; and even as we try to allow God's pure love to be seen through us, because we are not perfect means that, in part, we fail. It underlines the fact that of ourselves we are poverty stricken in the realm of love.

To see the total love that we may expect to enjoy in heaven we need only look at Jesus as he is seen in the gospels. Bryant reminds us "In him we see love not in the splendour and joy of heaven but in the darkness and selfishness of earth". If true love is in short supply we need to learn, with the Spirit's help, to give and receive it, and to outwork it in our lives.

That God loves mankind is due not to man being so irresistibly lovely, lovable and loving, but because it is in the nature of God to love, whether the object of his love is lovely or not.

D. Stuart Briscoe

These words tell us that we are loved even when we are undeserving of love. The manifestation of that love through Christ dying for sin on the cross proves this, for he was dying for a people who were dead in sin, a people who rejected him then and who still reject and crucify him afresh today.

As we look into our hearts we may wonder at the nature of a God who can love the kind of people that we sometimes are. For there are times when we turn aside from following closely. We sometimes say and do things which are unloving. We know that we are undeserving of his love; a love that is shown in his mercy toward us. Because he is God he continues to love us and to desire our good.

Having accepted that Christ's death was for us we need to be aware of the enormity of a love that acted on behalf of a world that could not be pleasing to God. This being so, John writes, "God loved the world so much that he gave his only Son, so that everyone who believes in him will have not destruction but eternal life."

[God] calls us to share our lives both with him and with one another in love.

David Watson

The call to follow God is a personal one but we are not alone in following him. Nor are we meant to tread the path on our own. We are a group, seeking separately and corporately to be true disciples of Christ. The call to love God is followed by the command to love our neighbour. We are to love God and also our fellow Christians, we are meant to show support and help to those who are on the road with us, and to receive the same from them.

Being a disciple means entering into warfare against the forces of evil, and we are better able to do this in the strength and unity of fellow believers. Their prayers uphold us, and we have to be mindful of their needs so that we may give them the same help.

Because we have each entered the family of God we are bound in love to each other to share the common life of discipleship. We each have the Spirit of God within us, we have been bought with the same price. The ties that bind us together cause us to be as servants one to the other.

He that loves God seeks neither gain nor reward, but only to lose all, even himself.

John of the Cross

" 'No man can serve two masters', and therefore in order not to lose God, he loses all that is not God'', says John of the Cross.

God is a jealous God in that he wants us for himself. He knows that our true satisfaction can only be found in him. It is only as we discard the things in life that hinder us that we can find that satisfaction, and we can only desire it when we love God for all that he is.

In this life much can become important to us, making a success of our lives, making money, having power. All of these enter into life in some way, whether in a big or smaller way. It is when they become the greater part of life that we need to question our love for God. If he is at the centre of our life then we desire only to please him.

We then have to face up to dispensing with those things that hinder our progress into a real knowledge of God. We have to take on a singleness of purpose, one of serving God alone. We have to "lose our life", that which is concerned with self, and seek God for himself. To love God means desiring him alone and being willing for all else to go.

It is God's will that I should see myself as bound to him in love as if all that he has done he has done for me alone.

Julian of Norwich

The timid heart, the gentle person or even the angry or aggressive one, may be unable to understand the extent of God's love towards them. Even believing that God is love may not allow them to appropriate it on a personal level for themselves. Life can bring hurts that make us feel that we are of little consequence, either to ourselves, to others or certainly to God. But God actually sees us as individuals, he knows our name and everything about us. He loves each one of us for ourselves.

It is when we grasp this that we can truly enter into a relationship with him. As I begin to realize that he loves "me", just as I am, then my love for him grows and our mutual love constitutes a bond that takes us on together.

It is not easy to take in the wonder of the fact that the plan of salvation would still have been undertaken even if it were only for me. Redemption reveals the love of God for me. The inheritance that comes from being redeemed is mine. We grieve him when we fail to understand how much he loves us and longs for our love.

Divine love is perfect peace and joy . . .

William Law

God's love is perfection. It is shown to us through Christ, and through him we know the divine love. It is God's love that reaches down to us and reveals our need of him. It is his love that has hewn out the path that leads us to himself, it is his love which saves us from sin.

He does not leave us to be alone, his love is continually working on our behalf, within us and in our circumstances. He seeks to impart himself to us so that the perfectness of love may be ours. Love is a quietness which embodies deep satisfaction. Love is in the peace which he imparts to us, in the joy that is ours through belonging to him.

Love overcomes all disquiet, all murmuring. It takes away resentment, refuses to accuse, is not disappointed. Love of itself desires nothing; and as the Spirit of Love is allowed to take over in our life so will these things die away. Our desire will be to accept God's love and to reveal it by all means so that it may be more and more known in the world.

Love is the highest gift of God; humble, gentle, patient love.

John Wesley

It is as we read the thirteenth chapter of 1 Corinthians that we really begin to understand the meaning of love. How it must be a part of everything that we do, and enter into all our thinking. Love is not just an emotion, a good feeling toward some of the people around us, it has to be upheld by an act of will. We must determine to accept the gift of love and to use it well.

Love makes us humble, gentle with other people, respecting them and what is theirs. Love, St Paul says, is kind, it is patient. It believes in people, is not glad when someone goes wrong. It can stand any kind of treatment and does not regard anyone as hopeless. Nothing, he says, can break love's spirit.

Whatever we may set our heart on being for God, it will be nothing without love. Paul is emphatic that we can be the most wise person and able to do the most wonderful things, but without love it is of no good to us.

This should be our aim, writes John Wesley, "nothing more but more of [this] love". This says Paul is "the most excellent way".

Real love means standing firm on God's principles of holiness.

Floyd McClung

We have to love as God would love but we also need to remember that God is holy. Holiness, like love, is an attribute of God and we should hunger after it as much as we seek to love. Our love for others should also be based on the desire that they might know the outworking of the Holy Spirit in their lives. Not only must we take care that we do not cause others trouble or to stumble, but we sometimes have to be strong in our attitudes to those who would depend too much on us.

Holiness means being clear on the question of sin, both in our own life and in the lives of others; love desires the best for them and it means that we cannot allow others to manipulate us. The desire to be pitied, to use a confidence as a hold, or to make circumstances a demand for help, are situations with which Christians can be faced, but as Floyd McClung says "Real love . . . must also be tough".

It means using love and prayer to set the situation straight, and to have a heart that desires to see holiness in others as well as pursuing it for ourselves.

Entrance . . . to the Holy Spirit's school of loving is through prayer.

Delia Smith

It is in prayer that we come to know God and therefore to know love. The more we realize his love for us so do we want to return that love. It is as we pray that God is able to teach us about himself and we learn about ourselves. We learn that we have a value, that we are lovable in the sight of God, and we even learn to love ourselves.

As we are able to love ourselves so there is a new confidence and freedom and we can reach out to others. Our continuing relationship with God enables the fruit of the Spirit to grow in our lives, which in itself is a witness to love. Prayer enables us to understand situations with the mind of God, to discern the needs of others, to want to use love for him in helping those around us.

We learn about reconciliation, and want to see peace between men and nations. We see that God loves sinners and realize that he desires that *all* shall come to him. We see that forgiveness is the outworking of love, and as God forgives so must we. We see that love is everything.

The standard of the husband's love is to be the cross of Christ.

John Stott

The way that marriage is thought about today is very different from even a comparatively short time ago. Couples are now much more inclined to make up their own rules within the relationship — rules which sometimes work and at other times do not.

If we look at the Scriptures we see that Paul tells husbands to love their wives, and this statement is more or less taken for granted as normal. However, that is only a part of the statement, for he goes on to say, "just as Christ loved the Church". This puts a husband in an extreme position — for Christ loved his bride unto death.

It seems that the husband has to care for his wife with the same love with which Jesus loves his Church. He must care for her, cherish her, and devote himself to her good. Stuart Briscoe writes of this passage in Ephesians, "This means that the husband will gladly make himself a servant of his wife to the extent he can bring enrichment to her in every possible way."

"Husbands, love your wives . . ." therefore means that the same love must be shown as Jesus shows towards his Church.

This love continues through death into eternity.

David Prior

David Prior is here commenting on the love of God and he is thinking of the words of St Paul in 1 Corinthians: "Love never ends". "This", he says, "is the love of God." How wonderful it is to be reminded that God loves us and goes on loving us.

A woman recently said of her son who had committed some crime and been sent to prison, "He's my son, this doesn't alter anything". Some people find that wrong-doing on the part of their children makes a great difference. They even refuse to acknowledge them as their children, and try to go on as if they had not been born. Others grieve over their children, feel their pain, long for them to be liberated from all that is holding them, are willing to forgive time and time again. Theirs is a continuing love, and in the way that it is shown, is a reflection of the love of God.

Paul, however, is writing for Christians, and he is expecting us to love one another with the love that is shed abroad in our hearts by the Holy Spirit — the love that does not change or fail.

In all this I was deeply moved with love for my fellow Christians, and longed for them to see and know what I had seen.

Julian of Norwich

Julian was a mystic who lived in the fourteenth century, and when she was thirty she received sixteen visions, writing about them in *Revelations of Divine Love*. The visions made a very deep impression on Julian and she longed that others should be comforted by what she had seen. Her heart was filled with love towards those who also loved Christ.

Love for our fellow Christians should extend further than mere loving or being concerned for their welfare. We should long to see them "bearing fruit in every good work" and "growing in the knowledge of God". Our "fellowship" with each other should lead to the sharing of spiritual truths; to an opening up of the knowledge of the ways of God to one another. Moving forward with God should be as much a priority in our love and desire for others as it is for ourselves.

It is in prayer that we can hold up to God our brothers and sisters in Christ, and that our love and longings for them find expression. As the Holy Spirit guides us in our thinking so can we work with him for their support and enlightenment, as we would long that others pray for us.

He showed me that all my preaching, writing and other ministry was absolutely *nothing* compared to my love-relationship with him.

David Watson

David Watson heard in January 1983 that he had cancer, and in February 1984 he died. He was very well known as a Christian leader and preacher, and travelled widely. Near the end of his life God spoke to him in a particular way, showing him that it was his love-relationship with God that was important. For the fact was that he had been so busy after his operation that God had been squeezed out.

It is easy to believe that God is more concerned with what we do for him than in having an intimate relationship with us. The truth is far different. He wants love to be reciprocated and to grow out of a personal relationship with himself. This only happens when time is spent together and made a priority.

The central part of our Christian life should be God himself. We shall know this is not so when our thoughts are taken up with what we are doing, for God is then being pushed out to the periphery. Nothing is as important as time spent with God, for out of what we learn from him comes the way in which we live our life.

Intercessory love "engages" the world to God, rather in the way that we engage the gears of a car to give it driving force.

Sister Margaret Magdalen CSMV

If we are to consider the praying in love for others then we need only remind ourselves that Jesus "is for all time able to save those who come to God through him, for he is always alive to intercede with God for them". He is continually mediating and praying for us, and we can only believe that in his desire for our welfare, love and pain are mingled.

We may know something of this love as we bear the burdens of others up in prayer to God. If we love God then we must be as concerned for them as he is, and this will include groups of people, nations, situations, as well as individuals. If we take them upon our hearts then we shall feel their sorrow and understand their pain, and out of this will come the desire that they may be free. Not necessarily free of their outward circumstances but the freedom that comes from their wanting God's will to be done in their lives.

If we examine the prayers of Jesus we can see how he understood the needs of those for whom he prayed. Our intercessory prayer, fuelled by love, will also seek to discern the true need and hold it up to God.

Power for the purpose of advancing reputations or inflating egos is not power motivated by love.

Richard Foster

"There is", says Richard Foster, "a power that destroys. There is also a power that creates."

The power that creates is the power that is used for good, that is put into the hands of God for him to use for the advancement of his kingdom. It is a power that is motivated by love for others and is guided by the Holy Spirit. Through this power great things can be accomplished, because it is not used for selfish ends, but comes from a humble loving heart.

Jesus was sometimes tempted through others to use his power in what he knew was a wrong way. He always resisted using it when it was for himself. It is a temptation that comes to men and women, for their own advancement or to boost a sense of importance. It comes from vanity and pride and a desire for honour and more assets, and springs from the ego.

The power that we need is the power from God, a power that is used as he ordains, that brings glory to him, that helps others and enables us to show the signs of belonging to him. It is power backed by love.

Jesus calls his followers to love, to love one another as he loves them; not just to love others as one loves oneself.

Jean Vanier

Jean Vanier writes that we can only love others like Jesus if we have an experience of his love. His love is shown not only by his willingness to die for us but by the love that is diffused by that death. He showed his love but he also gives us his love. Because through him we are free — liberated — then we are less self-centred. Our desire now is to do his will; and with our trust in him, we are able to love others as he loves them.

We love ourselves and doubtless are blinded, but the love of God is a love which is clearsighted, a love which seeks the best for us at all times. It means that loving as he does may make us vulnerable; that we have to see as he sees and with the same understanding. Implicit in this love is that of giving it to those who, on a human level, may appear to be unlovable.

To love as Jesus loves means forgetting self; seeing the good in others; acting in their best interests; loving in spite of what is unlovely. It means staying very close to Jesus to learn of his love.

In love he wants to encourage you, fill you, provide for you.

Colin Urquhart

God's love is not static; a trap which we may unconsciously fall into. We understand that God is love and imagine that it is rather like being enveloped. God's love is active, entering every part of our lives. To grasp this fully we have to believe that his love is personal. He loves each one of us as individuals, and everything that is of concern to us, concerns him. There is nothing about us that is not of interest to him, and it adds to the building up of the relationship when we allow ourselves to commit the small as well as the large things to him.

Committal is an important action, because it is as we let him into even the things that are not necessarily spiritual that we see how he can provide in a material sense.

When we admit to bad temper, inability to cope, frustration, lack of love toward others; because we know he loves and cares, we can believe that he will be active on our behalf.

God is continually telling us in Scripture of his love. We have to believe what he says and allow him to show us that he longs to provide for us in every way.

In my search for gospel peace I have no option as a Christian but to love and to strive hard to like everyone, irrespective of class, colour or creed.

Michael Buckley

Jesus said we must love not only those who love us, but that we must love our enemies. "If you love those who love you, what reward will you get?" To love our enemies, those who would harm us, or those who dislike us, is not at all easy; at the very least we would rather ignore them. We must also learn not to dislike nations, denominations, groups of people; those whom we would disparage.

Rejection of any overture does not let us off the hook. We have to continue to love. Anything less means that we are still tending to think only of ourselves rather than trying to reveal God through our life. Not only this, but as Michael Buckley suggests, if we wish to see peace in the world, then we must seek to make peace with all who are within our own small world.

The more we allow ourselves to be open to God's love, so shall we be more inclined to want to love others. As we genuinely try to understand people, so will the barriers come down and peace come into the situation, and we shall be blessed as God's peacemakers.

Love is extravagant in the price that it is willing to pay.

Joni Eareckson Tada

Dogs nowadays are able to have these wonderful leads enabling their owners to have them on a short lead when walking in a congested area or to run free in more open spaces. We sometimes see something like this in a family, where a child is not allowed to leave the shelter of the home. Even in adult life the "short lead" is still being used in the name of love, when true love is willing to let go.

It is said that if we release our children then we always keep them; if we try to keep them, then in essence we lose them. Normally we want the best for our children but it cannot be on our terms. Love for them will be shown in understanding, in making sacrifices. "Love never thinks in terms of 'how little', but always in terms of 'how much' ", writes Joni.

Love does not have boundaries; it does not say "so far and no further". It goes "overboard" in the extravagance of giving. Wherever we love that love should be shown by our desire to forget cost to ourselves. Our example is God himself who gave all in giving his Son.

We shall not in the end be judged by our gifts or our learning, but by our love, our likeness to Christ.

Michael Green

If we want to know about love we must read what Paul says in the New Testament. In 1 Corinthians 13 he tells us of "the most excellent way" of love. We are warned that we can have so much that appears to be spiritually sound, but if love is not in any of it then it is as nothing.

Love has to be in so much of us and our thinking that it permeates every part of what we do and how we react. It has to be there in our home, in the work-place, in our place of worship. In whatever situation we find ourselves we are to meet it with love. This can seem difficult in the midst of the bickering, backbiting, struggle for power, and all the difficulties that can arise.

It is in showing love in and through our circumstances that we reveal Christ. As we forgive others we are showing Jesus to them. Paul tells us in Romans that God pours out his love into our hearts by the Holy Spirit. As we ask the Spirit to give us this love so we shall find it rules in our lives.

Our experiences of love can tell us something about God's love for us.

Basil Hume

Love at its best reveals how God loves us. The way our parents love us; love within the family group; how our friends love us; the marriage partnership. We see love not only as it is given to us but as we respond and return that love. We can be hurt by love, and it can make us suffer.

In a human relationship we find that as we begin to receive love from a person so does our heart warm towards them. As we begin to understand something of God's love for us so too we begin to open up to him. The more we realize how great is his love then the more we want to love him in return.

It is true that we may have been hurt by human relationships, but God's love is a perfect love. We may grieve him but we must hold fast to the certainty of a love towards us that does not change. Even when it would seem that we cannot sense his love in the dire circumstances of the moment, it is still there.

To love God means to trust him and hang on to the knowledge that God loves each one of us.

The vision of God means the vision of Love.

Robert Llewelyn

The candle in the window each night or the yellow ribbons tied to the branches of a tree are the symbols of a love that flows out from a father/mother's heart. A love that yearns for its child whatever it has done or however far way it has gone. In the Bible story of the prodigal son we see love in action. We know that Jesus told this parable of the son who came back home after a life of dissipation, to show how God loves.

The Bible says, "While he was still a long way off, his father saw him. . . ." It isn't hard to imagine that day after day the father looked out for his son. That whatever he was doing his thoughts would be on whether the boy would come back that day.

Jesus told other parables that revealed his Father's love and deep care for each of us. Even as we turn away from "home" and wend our way to the equivalent of the big city God's love follows and stays with us. When we can bear no more and turning look upon Love, we find not anger but only a welcome.

We find rest in those we love and we provide a resting place in ourselves for those who love us.

Bernard de Clairvaux

We sometimes feel that we have nothing in ourselves that can be of use to others, but our love is perhaps the greatest thing that we can give. We can, as Bernard de Clairvaux says, "provide a resting place".

Although it may be natural to go to those who we know love us when things are not going so well, we also find "rest" when we just enter the company of those whom we love and who love us. The very knowledge that we are loved appears to act on our whole being as we relax together. We find freedom in exploring ideas, in opening up to one another.

It is not easy for some to show love in a demonstrative way. It is revealed instead by acceptance of a person, by being available, by allowing the other to be himself and not needing to keep the mask on. It does not necessarily mean being together; the very thought of those we love and who love us can sustain us at all times.

Love is a part of the God who *is* Love. It comes from unexpected sources and we may give it where there is little response; but giving provides something for the other person as receiving it does for us.

To be sure we are loved by God and to be able to help others to be sure — that is our vital, inner resource for the human journey and our service in the world.

Mark Gibbard SSJE

The world is full of sad people who not only do not know the love of God but feel unloved by other human beings. Circumstances may have separated them from family or difficult situations caused a withdrawal into a life of loneliness and the belief that nobody cares. Others may feel completely contented with their life and do not think that there is anything else that could enhance it.

Mark Gibbard believes that we all need the divine friendship as much as we need human companionship. That knowing God can not only bring something very wonderful into our own life, but that we then have something of value to give to others.

As Christians, sure of the love of God, we should be maturing in that love by reason of our growing closeness to him. It is that closeness that causes his love to be revealed and reaches out to those who do not know God. It is a part of being loved by God that we should also help other people to come to know of the love of God for them. The strength that we have found can be shown to be for all. To help others in this is a part of our human journey.

The root of Christian love is not the will to love, but the faith that one is loved by God.

Thomas Merton

To fall in love means that life becomes very attractive and everything seems wonderful. It even allows us to look on our fellow human beings in a benign way. How much more can we feel confidence and love towards others, when we realize the tremendous love that God bears towards us.

It is out of the knowledge that we ourselves are loved that we can love others. To know that we are deemed lovable means a great deal. To understand how that love was shown and what it cost makes us humble. What it should also do is to make us more understanding of other people, realizing that we are all those who have sinned in the eyes of God. If we have found forgiveness, then it is out of the knowledge of God's love for us that we can love others.

Have you ever stopped really to think about the love of God for you? The wonder of the Almighty One being concerned about one person and the gift of the ability to believe in that love? Faith — belief — trust in God means that out of that security we are able to give ourselves to others.

When I show love toward others, I know that it is Jesus who is acting within me.

St Therese of Lisieux

Many of us are not naturally loving, yet if we are to obey the command that Jesus gave us, we have to find love for others and to show it to them.

In fact, that love can only come from Jesus himself. We have to draw love from him in order to feel love for those around us. We need to learn from him. It starts by thinking positively, looking for the good in people rather than concentrating on what we may feel are their bad points. It means acting love towards them.

Then, we must continually draw near to the source of love, Jesus himself. As we come to know him, so we know his mind and take on something of his nature. We become more open to him, desire to please him, allow him to work through us. So it is that his love can flow from him to others and we can find that we are able genuinely to care for people.

Jesus asks us to love others even as he loves them. He does not ask of us anything that is not possible for us. The more we become one with him the more we shall love.

Mother-love asks nothing for self.

Ruth Burrows

Ruth Burrows in her writing speaks of "the fount of all maternal love — God himself".

However we may feel concerning the gender question and God, whether we shudder at the thought of calling God "Mother", we must concede that from God come the sensitive motherly emotions that are a part of the make-up of his creatures.

An illustration given by Ruth Burrows is a translation from the French: "A son has torn the heart out of his mother's breast because his loved one wanted it. Turning away he stumbles and drops the heart, and the mother's heart anxiously asks, 'Did you hurt yourself, my child?' "

Self-giving may well be a large part of motherhood but this itself comes from the God who made us in his image. It is a love that gives continually and loves in spite of what her child does. A mother feels for her child, tends it in sometimes sad and heartrending circumstances, loves even when there appears to be no return of that love. This is love as God himself loves; by looking at a mother and her child we can see something of the love that God has for us.

At the crossroads of every decision, I must ask only this: "What is the loving thing to do?"

John Powell SJ

John Powell believes that the loving person does not ask primarily about money or pleasure, but that the basic drive is simply to be a loving human being. This automatically leads to the question of "What is the loving thing to do?"

Love does not necessarily mean being soft, or doing what the loved one wants all the time. True love wants the best for the person concerned and this may mean appearing to be hard.

God himself disciplines his children, but it is done out of the abundance of his love for them. Loving parents will seek to do the best for their children, weighing up the options. To have a child on drugs can mean condoning or against its desire having it placed in care, for rehabilitation. Love sometimes has to be tough, even allowing suffering, when this is for another's good.

We have all seen the "love" which excuses all kinds of behaviour; and we have also seen the results of this type of love. This love has turned someone into a selfish person incapable of offering love and consideration in their turn, expecting always that others will pander to their whims. True love means commitment.

When we say that God loves us we mean that he cares for each single one of us as if there is no one else for him to care for.

Michael Ramsey

We find it difficult to understand the breadth of the love of God and at the same time taper it down to love for each individual. Even more difficult may be comprehension of a love that embraces "me" as one of those individuals. I know that I am a person, that I am "one", but can it truly be possible that God's love envelops me totally? That his care for me is as if there were no others?

It is when we fail to grasp this truth, or having believed it, begin to have doubts, that darkness descends upon us. We begin to sink as did Peter when he walked on the water. As he realized that he was no longer in control, but sinking, Peter cried out to the Lord, who immediately caught hold of him.

Throughout Scripture God reveals his love for the individual and we read over and over again of this love. If we need more we only have to look at the salvation plan. The door to God is through the cross, the fact of having gone through should be sufficient to understand that his love is personal for everyone who goes through to meet him.

Very few people know that they are loved without conditions or limits.

Henri Nouwen

Nouwen suggests that the need in our world is for men and women who know the heart of God and who are able to show it to others.

Simon Peter is revealed to us in the New Testament as a man who could be both weak and strong. He could be naive and yet at times have great insight. When Jesus commissioned Peter, he asked him "Do you love me?"

It may be that it did not seem as if Peter answered the question very satisfactorily, yet he did become a great Christian leader. Along the way he understood that loving Jesus meant knowing him, and in that knowledge he was able to become a shepherd to the sheep.

The love of God is a love that is completely unchangeable — there are no shadows. To love God is to enter into a relationship where one is loved completely. This is the essential message of the Gospel and the world needs to understand from us that God's love is something which can be relied upon with certitude; but it often has to be seen in his followers before it can be understood.

The poor are great people worthy of love.

Mother Teresa

112

Mother Teresa's work among the very poor is well known. It is a work that many of us must feel that we could never attempt. The poor are helpless, they have nothing to give, and what is given to them is given knowing that it must be done with an entirety that brings no return on a human level. It is done in love because of Christ, to please him, allowing self to be used that he might show his love to those who have no hope.

Poverty means being without what we feel are the necessities of life: food, warmth and shelter, the kind of poverty that is rarely seen in the West. There is, however, another kind of poverty: that of being unloved, unwanted, misunderstood — a poverty that can be found everywhere.

To go day after day without a kindly word. To be old and disregarded or to be young and dismissed as without worth; this, too, is poverty.

It is into these circumstances that we may go with the gift of love. Not as a bountiful people, but first offering ourselves to God, that his love may be seen as we in turn offer it humbly to those who are in need.

Falling in love with God can be very similar to falling in love with a human being.

Lionel Blue

Falling in love is full of excitement. It has been called an illness and certainly there are many recognizable symptoms and a feeling of dis-ease. When we meet God these same exciting feelings often take place. We want to be with the loved one, our thoughts are of him, there is a churning up feeling inside. Our desire is to please, and to know more about this wonderful person.

Perhaps it is good that this preliminary feeling gradually changes, both on a human level and as time extends, also in our relationship with God. As two people grow in knowledge of each other there should be new discoveries to share, and love deepens and becomes stronger. There is more understanding of the way in which life has to be lived together.

There may well be dull periods, but then there are also still exciting moments. There are days of shared pain but others of joy; and underlying all, the knowledge of belonging and being entirely "at home" with each other. We fall into human love, and if we are fortunate there is a happy progress. True union with God is sure of a happy ending.

We can only really love with a universal heart as we discover that we are loved by the universal heart of God.

Jean Vanier

The person who knows little of love will find difficulty in giving love to others, and will be suspicious when asked to receive it. It is when love is truly understood as being free from conditions, as something which is willingly given, that it can begin to warm the cold heart.

Even if we are capable of love, it is usually limited to those who are lovable. There are many who for one reason or another do not attract love. Each time that we deny love it is as if we turn away from God; we leave his side as *he* loves the broken one.

The ultimate giving in love is told in John 3. Because God loved, he gave his Son. It was not as if the Son was given for something good and beautiful. He was given for a dark and sinful people, yet it was a perfect love that suffered.

As we look at our own hearts, become aware of thoughts and actions that need to be hidden, we realize that God's love is indeed our salvation. As we accept his love, we find that love reaching out to others through us, as we see ourselves accepted we learn to accept others.

Christian love grants the beloved all his imperfections and weaknesses.

Søren Kierkegaard

Kierkegaard reminds us in his writings that if Christian love were not unchangeable, and that it loved in spite of the changes seen in a person, Christ would never have loved for he could not have found a perfect man.

The love of God is a pure, unselfish love. A love that does not cease because the loved one would seem to be unworthy of love. If we are to love others as we are loved by God, we have to take hold of God's love, understand what it is and then seek to love as he loves.

As we look at God-made-man we begin to see love; a love that continues to love when it is betrayed and denied. Christians are meant to love in this same way, seeking to love the essential person behind all the faults and imperfections.

How can we do this? Perhaps by remembering that we are loved by God in spite of our imperfections, of which we are usually fully aware. By meditating on the nature of God's love and seeking to become like Christ, for the way in which we accept God's love, how we love him and love others, are bound up together.

Love, especially in the hospice context, can be a very practical and earthly business.

Sheila Cassidy

In her book *Sharing the Darkness*, Sheila Cassidy shares the fact that love in the context of the mutilated and dying is not a sweet and sentimental thing. Love in this type of circumstance can be difficult, it has to go beyond the ravished body and reach down to the person that is inside the twisted form. Love in this context means coping with the undignified things of terminal illness but at the same time allowing the person to retain dignity.

Neither is it just a matter of treating the body, there must surely be the duty in love, to tend to the needs of the inner person. So often we forget that here is someone who thinks and feels, hurts and grieves just as we do; but it is not easy to love when we perhaps feel disgust and revulsion.

For those of us who have to come to terms, either with the sick, or with the mentally or physically disabled, we can remember that the Spirit of the Father is in all of his children. Realizing this helps in reaching out to the other one and liberates the love within us. It enables us to see the body as an adjunct to the life that is within.

If you find that you have truly kept the Lord's commands, then you may rest assured that you are one who loves the Lord.

Wong Ming-Dao

Wong Ming-Dao, a Chinese pastor, was imprisoned for twenty-three years for his faith. He believes that if our way of life does not harmonize with the Lord's commands, then we are deceiving ourselves concerning our love for God.

Love is not just a simple matter of saying "I love you". It has to be borne out by actions; by showing trust; by being faithful. In the hurly-burly of family life love is often shown by practical things: a meal on the table; helping with the chores, and generally seeking to please and to be considerate. Jesus said, "If you love me, you will obey my commands"; so that the very way in which we live our lives shows whether we have love for him or not.

We need to be upright in our dealings with others, free of jealousy and envy. We have to learn to esteem other people; to be ready to forgive; to care for others and to give out of our riches — or poverty. We have to seek the way of holiness. If we love God we will want to please him by being obedient, this is the way in which we show our love for him.

If we are looking for a definition of love, we should look not in a dictionary, but at Calvary.

John Stott

It is not known where the true site of the crucifixion is to be found, but as someone has said, it is not important to be sure. The crucifixion and resurrection have significance for us, where they happened does not. The fact of Calvary is the most important thing in history; the fact of Calvary is the most important thing in the lives of human beings if they will accept it as such. The greatest need of man was met at the cross and it is at the cross that we see the definition of love.

"For God loved the world so much that he gave his only Son, so that everyone who believes in him should have not destruction but eternal life", translates Barclay. Here is our salvation, but to see the love of God we need to understand the cost that was involved. Jesus "emptied himself" of his glory in coming down to earth. He identified with human beings, the sinners. He died ignominiously in their place outside the city in the company of thieves, hanging on a cross.

Separated from the Father this is the moment of greatest suffering; and it reveals pure love.

God's love to sinners reaches its objective as it brings them to know him in a covenant relation.

J.I. Packer

A covenant is a compact or agreement between two parties which involves dependence upon each other. As early as Genesis we read that God set up a covenant relation with Abraham. God Almighty (El Shaddai) came to him and said "This is my covenant with you", and this is also our inheritance. In becoming our God he gives himself so that in him we have everything that we need, as we in turn give ourselves to him.

God's love is shown in the giving of his Son to be our Saviour and we know that this love is for each one of us. It manifests itself in his care for our needs, but more than this, he promises that he will give of himself to us. So it is that we may draw on his mercy, his power, his wisdom, his grace. His all-sufficiency is available to each one of us as a part of a covenant relation.

We look at the cross and marvel that love could go through so much. The cross was necessary in order that we should be reconciled to God, but in his love God gives even more, he gives himself.